Greta Thunberg: Climate Activist

Hal Marcovitz

ReferencePoint Press®

San Diego, CA

© 2021 ReferencePoint Press, Inc.
Printed in the United States

For more information, contact:
ReferencePoint Press, Inc.
PO Box 27779
San Diego, CA 92198
www.ReferencePointPress.com

LIBRARY OF CONGRESS CATALOGING-IN-PUBLICATION DATA

Names: Marcovitz, Hal, author.
Title: Greta Thunberg : climate activist / By Hal Marcovitz.
Description: San Diego, CA : ReferencePoint Press, Inc., 2021. | Includes
  bibliographical references and index.
Identifiers: LCCN 2020005613 (print) | LCCN 2020005614 (ebook) | ISBN
  9781682829233 (library binding) | ISBN 9781682829240 (ebook)
Subjects: LCSH: Thunberg, Greta, 2003---Juvenile literature. | Child
  environmentalists--Sweden--Biography--Juvenile literature. |
  Environmentalists--Sweden--Biography--Juvenile literature.
Classification: LCC GE56.T58 M37 2021 (print) | LCC GE56.T58 (ebook) |
  DDC 363.738/74092 [B]--dc23
LC record available at https://lccn.loc.gov/2020005613
LC ebook record available at https://lccn.loc.gov/2020005614

Contents

Greta Thunberg: *Time*'s Person of the Year

Each December since 1927, *Time* magazine—a mainstay of American culture—has selected a newsmaker as its "Person of the Year." This is an honor bestowed on an internationally known figure who the magazine believes has made the greatest impact on life during the preceding twelve months. Over the past century, among those chosen for the honor have been American presidents as well as other world leaders, noted scientists, astronauts, military leaders, corporate executives, and religious leaders.

In December 2019, *Time* shocked its readers when it selected for its Person of the Year not a president, scientist, or general, but a sixteen-year-old girl from Sweden: Greta Thunberg. "Meaningful change rarely happens without the galvanizing force of influential individuals, and in 2019, the earth's existential crisis found one in Greta Thunberg," wrote *Time* editor in chief Edward Felsenthal. "Thunberg has become the biggest voice on the biggest issue facing the planet."[1]

Combating Climate Change

The issue in which Thunberg has immersed herself is climate change: the gradual and consistent warming of the earth's atmosphere caused by the widespread in-

dustrialization of the planet. This industrialization has resulted in the production of gases (such as carbon dioxide)
that trap heat in the atmosphere and
cause the earth to warm. According
to the National Aeronautics and Space
Administration (NASA), the earth's atmosphere has grown warmer by 1.4°F

> "Meaningful change rarely happens without the galvanizing force of influential individuals, and in 2019, the earth's existential crisis found one in Greta Thunberg."[1]
>
> —Edward Felsenthal, *Time* magazine editor in chief

(0.8°C) since 1880. That may sound like a minor increase but it is
not. Nearly all of the world's scientists agree that climate change
has had—and will continue to have—a severe impact on life on
earth. Climate change, also known as global warming, is seen as

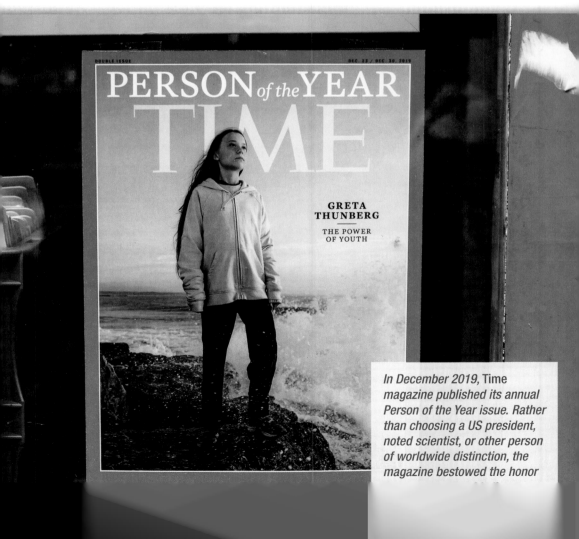

In December 2019, Time *magazine published its annual Person of the Year issue. Rather than choosing a US president, noted scientist, or other person of worldwide distinction, the magazine bestowed the honor*

the cause of melting polar icecaps, severe storms, blazing hot summers, wildfires, the flooding of coastal cities, and the disappearance of species of plant and animal life. And yet, even though scientists have been warning about the catastrophes that could be caused by climate change for several decades, governmental leaders have done relatively little to address the problem. Many governmental leaders fear that reining in the industries and lifestyles responsible for warming the planet's atmosphere would severely impact the economies of their nations, leading to job loss, poverty and other ills.

In the face of this inaction, Thunberg's activism to combat climate change has ignited a spark—particularly among teens and other young people. It will, after all, be the people of Thunberg's generation who may be most affected by climate change. Many fear that when they reach their adult years, cities will be on their way to becoming unlivable and severe weather will become a way of life. "We can't continue living as if there was no tomorrow, because there is a tomorrow," declares Thunberg. "That is all we are saying."[2]

Certainly, many world leaders, environmental activists, and scientists have led campaigns to address the causes of climate change, but Thunberg—fed by her spirit and fueled by youthful energy—has brought a dynamic passion to the crusade. She launched her campaign to convince world leaders to take definitive action to curb climate change in 2018 when she started carrying a hand-painted sign in Stockholm, Sweden's capital. The images of the lone schoolgirl protesting against climate change spread throughout her country and then throughout the rest of Europe, and then to virtually all countries on earth.

> "We can't continue living as if there was no tomorrow, because there is a tomorrow."[2]
>
> —Greta Thunberg

Those images were soon punctuated by the fiery speeches Thunberg delivered to rallies as well as meetings of political leaders—most notably a session of the United Nations (UN) General

Assembly in New York City in 2019. "For more than 30 years the science has been crystal clear," Thunberg told the UN delegates. "How dare you continue to look away, and come here saying that you're doing enough when the politics and solutions needed are still nowhere in sight."[3]

Youngest Person of the Year

Thunberg's emotional crusade has ignited a campaign to address climate change among young people across the planet. Rallies demanding action on climate change are now common in cities in North America, Europe, Asia, and South America. Young people, not much older than Thunberg, are now running for public office, winning elections, and declaring climate change as the number one issue on their agendas.

After looking at the activism sparked by Thunberg, *Time*'s editors knew the Swedish teenager deserved the honor of Person of the Year. The issue of the magazine that hit newsstands on December 23, 2019, featured a portrait of Thunberg on its cover. The photograph depicted Thunberg standing on rocks slapped by ocean waves. The expression on her face can only be described as troubled. "She was a solo protestor with a hand-painted sign 14 months ago," said Felsenthal. "She's now led millions of people around the world, 150 countries, to act on behalf of the planet."[4]

Thunberg is by far the youngest person ever selected by *Time* as Person of the Year. In selecting a teen activist for this honor, *Time* was perhaps sending its own message about climate change: that young people have taken a stand on the issue, and world leaders would do well to listen to Thunberg and other young activists, because now is the time to seriously address the issue of climate change.

Chapter One

The Climate Crisis Comes to Stockholm

When Greta Thunberg was eleven years old, her teacher showed a video to her class on the effects of climate change. The video included images of widespread flooding and extreme weather events such as severe storms and stifling heat waves. There were images of starving polar bears and other animals. Those images deeply troubled Thunberg; she found herself in tears as the video flashed across the screen.

The video had an impact on others as well—most of the students were clearly in a sad mood when the video concluded. But her classmates moved on. They soon found themselves immersed in their studies or how to tackle that evening's homework, or what games to play at recess. Thunberg could not put those images out of her head. She fell into a deep depression—she spoke little, even to her family and friends. For months, she ate little. When she started suffering the effects of malnutrition—she lost 22 pounds (10 kg) in two months—her parents considered taking her to a hospital. Instead, her mother and father took time off from their jobs to stay home with Thunberg, nursing their daughter through her troubled time.

The video that had prompted tears and depression would continue to haunt Thunberg. As she entered

8

her teenage years, Thunberg continued to focus on images of the devastating effects of climate change reported on Swedish television and other media. In May 2018, at the age of fifteen, she won an essay contest sponsored by a Stockholm newspaper. The contest asked Stockholm students to express their feelings about climate change. Wrote Thunberg, "I want to feel safe. How can I feel safe when I know we are in the greatest crisis in human history?"[5]

Lessons Taught at Home

Thunberg is not the first member of her family to recognize the effects of climate change. She is distantly related to Svante Arrhenius, a chemist who in 1896 first signaled the effects that industrialization and pollution could have on the earth's climate. For his efforts, Arrhenius was awarded the Nobel Prize for Chemistry in 1903. The Nobel Prizes are an international honor conferred annually on scientists and others who make significant contributions to human civilization.

Thunberg was born January 3, 2003, in Stockholm. Her father, Svante Thunberg, is a noted Swedish television and stage actor. Thunberg's mother, Malena Ernman, is an opera singer who has also acted in Swedish films and television dramas. Thunberg's younger sister, Beata, was born in 2005. The four of them live together with their two dogs, Roxy and Moses.

Despite her parents' occupations that have often taken them on theatrical tours away from home, Thunberg's early years were largely normal and uneventful. But recognizing the importance of protecting the environment was a lesson taught repeatedly in the Thunberg home. During Sweden's cold winters, Thunberg would often find herself staring out the window as nearby factories belched smoke from their chimneys into the sky over Stockholm.

Thunberg recalls asking her mother, "Is smoke dirty?"

"Of course it is," responded Ernman.

"Then why does everyone do it?"[6] asked Thunberg.

Supporting Their Daughter

Thunberg heard similar messages in school. Her teachers were constantly telling their students about the importance of turning the lights off when leaving a room to save electricity, and to not waste water or food. When Thunberg asked her teachers why it was important to not be wasteful, she was told that being wasteful hurts the environment.

And so, when Thunberg fell into a state of depression following the video shown in her classroom, her parents responded by showing they, too, cared deeply about preserving the environment. They decided to support their daughter by taking several steps at home to do their part to protect the environment. They stopped serving meat during meals, becoming vegetarians and even growing their own vegetables in their backyard. The meat industry is regarded as a major contributor to climate change because in many places the land required for grazing has to be cleared of trees. Trees absorb carbon dioxide and, therefore, help scrub the atmosphere of an overabundance of this gas. Also, to

Greta Thunberg was just eleven years old when she learned about the disastrous effects of climate change. After watching a heartbreaking video in school that showed starving polar bears and other animals, she sank into a deep depression.

grow feed for animals, ranchers need to use copious amounts of fertilizer, which emits carbon dioxide.

Thunberg's parents installed solar panels on the roof of their home in Stockholm. The panels absorb energy from the sun and then convert it into electricity that is used in the home. Ernman, whose career on the opera stage took her across Sweden, elected to give up air travel and rely instead on trains to travel from city to city. Airliners, with their powerful jet engines, are regarded as the most environmentally damaging way to travel. Says Svante Thunberg, "We did it to make her happy and to get her back to life."[7]

Thunberg slowly emerged from her depression, but it was clear she was still troubled—and keenly focused on the effects of climate change. She continued to eat little. She stopped going to school—ultimately, she would not return to school for nearly a year. The Thunbergs feared their daughter suffered from the eating disorder known as anorexia. Teenagers and, in particular, teenage girls are often troubled by images of their bodies, believing themselves to be overweight. And so many anorexia sufferers often stop eating under the impression that they will ultimately resemble the slim and athletic models featured in advertisements and elsewhere in the media.

To find out whether their daughter did, in fact, suffer from an eating disorder, the Thunbergs took Greta, now just twelve years old, to the Stockholm Center for Eating Disorders, based at the Astrid Lindgren Hospital in Stockholm. At the center, she was interviewed by a staff psychiatrist who determined she was not anorexic but, instead, had a form of autism known as Asperger's syndrome.

Asperger's Syndrome

People with autism often have trouble communicating or otherwise interacting with others. There are varying degrees of autism. Some people are able to carry on normal lives; others need a lifetime of support from family members so that they can function in society. Thunberg's condition, Asperger's syndrome, is often characterized by deep levels of concentration. People with Asperger's syndrome can focus so intently on their own thoughts that they completely lose touch with what is going on around them.

Thunberg returned from the clinic. Immediately after arriving home she ate a green apple. Her diet soon consisted of rice, avocados, bananas, and pancakes. Her diet rarely changes. Even when it comes to what to have for lunch, Thunberg's thoughts are keenly focused and they rarely change.

Thunberg, who has described Asperger's syndrome as gift rather than as a disease, resolved to use her diagnosis as a force for change. She knew that going forward, she would concentrate on little else besides climate change. Finding ways to save the environment would dominate her thoughts. "I see the world in black and white, and I don't like compromising," Thunberg said. "If I were like everyone else, I would have continued on and not seen this crisis."[8]

Greenhouse Effect

Thunberg's belief that the crisis of climate change has largely been ignored over the years is quite accurate. The major alarms about climate change did not surface until 1988, when NASA climate scientist James E. Hansen testified before a US Senate hearing, telling legislators, "The greenhouse effect has been detected and is changing our climate right now."[9]

> "The greenhouse effect has been detected and is changing our climate right now."[9]
>
> —James E. Hansen, NASA scientist

The greenhouse effect—which is the cause of the warming planet—occurs due to the continual emission of carbon dioxide into the atmosphere. Carbon dioxide, a gas, is emitted during the burning of fossil fuels—coal, oil, and natural gas. The internal combustion engine that powers most of the world's automobiles operates by burning gasoline, a product refined from oil.

Advocates for Refugees

Greta Thunberg learned a lot about advocacy and activism from her parents. Before they took up the cause of climate change alongside their daughter, Thunberg's parents, actor Svante Thunberg and opera star Malena Ernman, were advocates for helping international refugees. The refugees were people who had been forced to leave their home countries because of warfare. In 2015, the Thunbergs invited a family of refugees from the Middle East nation of Syria to live in their vacation home on the Swedish island of Ingarö.

Syria has been embroiled in a civil war since 2011. Since then, some 7 million Syrians have fled their homeland. Many fled to European countries where governments and refugee advocacy groups have welcomed them. Sweden has been among the most welcoming of European nations, finding homes for about 110,000 Syrian refugees.

When a Syrian refugee family arrived in Sweden in 2015, the Thunbergs paid for their bus fare from Stockholm to Ingarö and turned their vacation home over to the family. Over the course of the next year the Thunbergs, along with daughters Greta and Beata, took many trips to Ingarö, helping the family members settle in Sweden until they were able to find a place of their own. Said Ernman, "We have a refugee situation in the world that is getting worse every month that goes by. . . . There are no simple solutions, but we cannot build a sustainable future with walls and barbed wire."

Quoted in Monir Loudiyi, "Malena Ernman on the New Refugee Act: 'Sad,'" *Göteborgs-Posten*, June 21, 2016. www.gp.se.

When carbon dioxide is released through the tailpipes of cars and trucks, it remains in the atmosphere, acting as a greenhouse gas. Carbon dioxide emissions trap the heat produced by the sun—much as a glass greenhouse traps heat, helping plants and flowers grow. As global temperatures rise, the effect on the environment includes extremely dry conditions, which have led to droughts and sparked wildfires. But the greenhouse effect also traps moisture in the atmosphere, which has resulted in severe

The rapid warming of the planet is occurring because of the greenhouse effect, in which carbon dioxide and other gasses trap and hold heat in the atmosphere. A major contributor is the burning of fossil fuels, including in the engines of the world's tens of millions of vehicles.

storms and flooding. Coastal cities in particular are exposed to the effects of climate change in the form of hurricanes of ever-increasing intensity.

Cars and trucks are not the only causes of greenhouse gases. Burning coal for fuel emits carbon dioxide. In 2020 the US Energy Information Administration (EIA) reported 589 coal-fired power plants producing electricity in the United States. Hundreds more are in operation across the globe. Natural gas, which also fuels power plants across the planet, also produces carbon dioxide when burned, though much less than coal does. According to the EIA, natural gas fuels 42 percent of the electricity production in the United States.

Bullied at School

Thunberg read about these facts and others in her school library — a place where she found a measure of refuge from an outside world she still found difficult to face. Following her diagnosis with Asperger's syndrome, Thunberg returned to school. To ease her depression, the psychiatrist at the Stockholm Center for Eating

Disorders prescribed an antidepressant drug to help lift her spirits. Thunberg did start to eat normally again but still spoke little to others, as she was often focused entirely on her own thoughts.

Back in school, Thunberg found her classmates unwilling to accept her unusual behavior. When they spoke to her, she either did not respond or answered them in a voice so low they could not understand her. She was often bullied. On one occasion, as Thunberg stepped out of the restroom at school, three girls stepped in front of her and beat her up. That afternoon, Thunberg returned home with cuts and bruises on her face and arms and a black eye.

To help Thunberg endure these troubling times, her parents reached out to the school, which agreed to make special accommodations for their daughter. A teacher was assigned to provide private lessons to Thunberg for two hours a day in the school library. Each day, her father dropped her off at the school entrance. She quietly made her way to the library, hoping to avoid the glares of her classmates. Afterward, her father picked her up at the school and they drove home.

Thunberg absorbed her lessons in the school library. She was an intelligent student. She has a photographic memory, meaning she can easily recall everything she reads or is taught. She scored well on the tests administered by her teacher. Still, though, she remained focused intently on the problem of climate change. She read every book in the school library on climate science and, eventually, came across a book written by Arrhenius.

Ice Ages

Thunberg learned that Arrhenius focused his studies on the ice ages, periods in the earth's history in which global temperatures drop, causing the expansion of glaciers across the surface of the planet. Scientists believe that during the past 1 million years, there have been at least five ice ages. Arrhenius wondered whether vast swings in the carbon content of the earth's atmosphere were responsible for changes in the planet's climate, both causing and curtailing the ice ages.

Arrhenius spent a year working out tedious calculations to determine how much sunlight is absorbed by the carbon gases present in the atmosphere. In 1896, he published a paper reporting that the carbon content of the atmosphere does have an impact on climate and that an increase could result in rising temperatures. Moreover, Arrhenius recognized that the Industrial Revolution—a time when the economies of major nations became more reliant on factory growth and less reliant on agriculture—was greatly fueling the emission of carbon dioxide into the atmosphere. At the time, most factories, office buildings, schools, and homes were heated by coal furnaces.

> "Our descendants, albeit after many generations, might live under a milder sky and in less barren surroundings than is our lot at present."[10]
>
> —Svante Arrhenius, Swedish chemist

Although Arrhenius received many honors for his study of climate change, including the Nobel Prize, he did not necessarily believe global warming was a bad idea. Living in Sweden, where the winters can be long and cold, Arrhenius believed a rise in global temperatures could eventually turn his homeland into something of a tropical paradise. He wrote, "We would then have some right to indulge in the pleasant belief that our descendants, albeit after many generations, might live under a milder sky and in less barren surroundings than is our lot at present."[10]

Worldwide Catastrophes

Arrhenius died in 1927, some six decades before Hansen issued his warning to the US Senate. Thunberg's ancestor did not foresee the worldwide catastrophes that could be caused by even the slightest change in global temperatures. According to the New York City–based Environmental Defense Fund (EDF), among the consequences that climate change has already caused across the earth are melting polar ice caps, a process which has caused chunks of ice to break away. That has reduced the size of the habitat for polar bears. One environmental group, Santa Monica,

Greta Thunberg's Flawless English

Anybody who has seen news broadcasts of Greta Thunberg speaking at rallies, addressing international meetings on climate change, or responding to questions from reporters must surely be struck by the fact that her English is flawless. After all, Thunberg is a native Swede, and Swedish is the language Thunberg has heard spoken by family members and friends her entire childhood.

Part of the reason for Thunberg's fluency in English certainly has to do with her intelligence—she has a photographic memory, which means her ability to recall virtually everything she has read and is taught is very powerful. Also, though, credit for her bilingual ability—her prowess at speaking two languages—goes to Sweden's school system.

In Swedish schools, English is a required course and taught to all students starting no later than the fifth grade. By the time Swedish students reach high school, they have the option of taking all their classes in English and to begin learning a third language, usually German, French, or Italian. Joanna Giota, director of education at the University of Gothenburg in Sweden, says Swedish officials have come to recognize English as a truly universal language, and Swedes know that to compete in the twenty-first-century economy they need to learn English. She says, "Sweden is . . . a country with a broad network of international trade and production relations. English is an international language with a broad geographic range. Thus, understanding the English language brings great advantages in many different contexts."

Joanna Giota, "Why Do All Children in Swedish Schools Learn English as a Foreign Language?," *System*, August 1995, p. 311.

California–based Global Animal, estimates that the worldwide population of polar bears has dropped by twenty thousand in recent years.

Raging wildfires are seen as another consequence of climate change. Rising temperatures tend to dry out the soil, plants, and trees—all of which helps spread wildfires. In 2018, some 8.5 million acres (34,400 square km) in the United States—an area of land the size of Maryland—were burned by wildfires.

Severe storms and flooding are also consequences of climate change. As huge swaths of land dry out due to warmer temperatures, the moisture in that land evaporates into the air. Warmer air can hold more moisture, and this greater amount of atmospheric moisture contributes to more powerful storms. Water expands when warmed, and warming oceans—along with the melting polar ice caps—are also the cause of rising sea levels. According to the US Environmental Protection Agency, since 1996 about 20 square miles (52 square km) of seashore along the Atlantic Coast have been lost to rising sea levels. That land is now underwater. For coastal cities, such as New York City, Miami, and Los Angeles, the implications of rising sea levels could be catastrophic: a federal agency, the US National Ocean Service, reports global sea levels could rise by nearly six feet by the end of this century—enough of a rise to totally submerge the city of Miami.

But while Arrhenius did not live to see such effects of climate change, his young descendant certainly has. While reading all she could about climate change in the school library, Thunberg re-

There are numerous harmful consequences of climate change. One of the worst is increasingly severe storms and flooding as evidenced by this flood in Spring, Texas, caused by Hurricane Harvey in 2017.

mained focused on the news and, more and more, saw evidence that the planet was changing—and not, as Arrhenius had predicted, for the good.

Thunberg soon turned to social media to tell the story of climate change. In 2018, at the age of fifteen, Thunberg established an Instagram account, often posting photographs she found on the internet of devastating floods as well as wildlife decimated by arid conditions. She also posted charts and graphs displaying scientific evidence of climate change. Even the photos she posted of herself, often accompanied by Roxy and Moses, carried a distinct message about the environment. The photos invariably depict Thunberg wandering through leafy forests, snowy hillsides, or sandy beaches, showing her intense passion for nature.

Hottest Summer on Record

As Thunberg was posting photos on her Instagram account, her homeland of Sweden was experiencing one of the hottest summers on record. Sweden is located in a region of northern Europe where the winters are long and the snowfall plenty. Ordinarily, a summer in Sweden is like early springtime elsewhere—it can be a bit chilly. Even in July and August, daytime temperatures in Sweden rarely exceed 73°F (23°C).

But in July 2018, record heat swept through Sweden and its neighboring countries, Norway, Denmark, and Finland. On one day in July, the high temperature in the city of Uppsala, a community near Stockholm, was reported at 93°F (34°C)—the hottest day recorded in Sweden in 262 years.

When severe weather afflicts a region, climate scientists are often quick to point out that extremes in daily weather are not necessarily a consequence of climate change. Weather is affected by many factors—the season of the year, wind direction, and moisture content of the atmosphere, among others. Therefore a region can experience very cold or very hot weather regardless of how much carbon dioxide may be trapping the sunlight. In the case of the northern European heatwave of 2018, however, scientists did point to climate change as a contributing factor. "We also shouldn't forget that the climate is already hotter," said Gustav Strandberg, a climate researcher at the Swedish Meteorological and Hydrological Institute. "The past 30 years have been clearly warmer than the average for the period as a whole."[11]

The hot weather caused more than an uncomfortably warm summer for Swedes and other residents of northern Europe. In addition to the hot temperatures, little rain had fallen in the region that summer. The dry conditions led to an outbreak of some sixty wildfires in a region of nearby Finland known as Lapland. The temperature that summer in Lapland hit a high of 86°F (30°C). Ordinarily, Lapland is covered year-round in a blanket of snow.

> "The past 30 years have been clearly warmer than the average for the period as a whole."[11]
>
> —Gustav Strandberg, climate researcher at the Swedish Meteorological and Hydrological Institute

Student Walkouts

Thunberg watched these events unfold around her, growing more troubled by the day. Newscasts showed the heroic efforts of firefighters in Lapland and Swedish teenagers frolicking on beaches that could have doubled for Southern California. All the while Thunberg wondered why nobody seemed to be doing anything about the climate crisis. One evening at dinner, she exploded in a rage, screaming at her parents, "I don't know if you realize it, there isn't much time. Burning stuff like heating oil and coal and fossil fuels are putting more and more carbon . . . into our atmosphere. It's being trapped because there is too much of the stuff and that is causing Earth to heat up. We need to do something."[12]

But there was another ongoing story in the news that year that caught her eye. In February 2018, nineteen-year-old Nikolas Cruz, who was later found to be suffering from a mental illness, opened fire with a semiautomatic rifle at Marjory Stoneman Douglas High School in Parkland, Florida, killing seventeen people, including fourteen students and three members of the faculty. Another seventeen people were injured by gunfire. A few weeks after the shooting, student activists started leading school walkouts to call attention to the lax gun control laws that enabled the mentally ill shooter to obtain a gun and use it against his classmates and teachers. The walkouts soon spread to schools throughout America.

News of the student walkouts and rallies garnered widespread media attention in America, but the headlines also made it across the ocean and were carried on news broadcasts in Europe. Thunberg saw that in America, young people were marching for a cause. She decided to do the same. If government leaders would not take action on their own to address climate change, it would be up to young people like her to force lawmakers to act.

Chapter Two

School Strike for the Climate

Swedish lawmakers meet to govern their country in a building known as the Riksdagshuset—in English, the Parliament House. The huge, ornate building was erected more than a century ago. Visitors approaching the building are greeted first by a row of towering concrete columns that stand across the front of the structure. On the morning of August 20, 2018, Greta Thunberg left her home in Stockholm, riding her bicycle across town to Parliament House. She wore a blue hoodie and leopard print pants. She sat down in front of the building on the hard cobblestone sidewalk. Thunberg propped a handmade sign against the wall of the Parliament House. The sign said, "Skolstrejk för klimatet." In English, the message translates to "School Strike for the Climate."

Thunberg decided not to go to school that day. In fact, she decided to stay out of school until September 9, 2018, the day of the Swedish election for seats in Parliament. She planned to protest the Swedish government's failure to address climate change.

At first, members of the Swedish parliament and others wandered by, most barely offering a glance to the lone teenager sitting next to her handcrafted sign. Some asked her why she wasn't in school. When she told them she was staging a school strike to save the climate, most shrugged their shoulders and kept walking. After a few hours she tried a new strategy. When she was asked the meaning of her sign, Thunberg launched into a brief speech

she hoped would alert people to the dangers of climate change. She also reminded them that an election was approaching—and to use their votes to support candidates who would take action on the issue of climate change. "Much of the world's population does not have the slightest idea what climate change means to us,"[13] she declared. Alas, her speeches didn't seem to raise much interest among passersby, either. Finally, at 3 p.m., she went home.

The Swedes Take Notice

Thunberg's school strike had been inspired by the students at Marjory Stoneman Douglas High School in Florida, who organized a national student walkout on April 20, 2018, to protest against ineffective gun control laws in America. Organized through numerous social media platforms, hundreds of thousands of students in all fifty states walked out of school that day. Thunberg's walkout was a solitary affair, but she was undaunted by the cool reception she received as she sat outside Parliament House on that first day. She returned the next morning and took her seat on the cobblestone sidewalk, again propping up her sign against the wall. This time she was approached by some news reporters who asked her what she was up to. Thunberg told the reporters she was staging a school strike to call attention to climate change. The reporters remained with her for several hours, watching as she again made pleas to members of Parliament and others as they walked by. Stories about Thunberg's campaign appeared in the next day's newspapers and other Swedish media. Soon, she found others joining her for the protest outside Parliament House. Within a few days, about forty

people had joined the protest. Stories about the growing protests were reported daily in the Swedish media.

Thunberg's climate strike gained attention with the help of social media as well. Starting with the first day of the strike she posted photos of herself, sitting in front of the Parliament House, on her Instagram and Twitter accounts. The message under the Instagram photo explained why she didn't go to school that day. It said, "We children don't usually do what you grown-ups tell us to do. We do as you do. And since you don't [care] about my future, I don't [care] either."[14] Others shared her posts. The posts soon came to the attention of Ingmar Rentzhog, a wealthy entrepreneur and environmentalist. He joined her at the protest and used his widespread influence on his Facebook and Twitter accounts to spread the message. Within a few days, some two hundred thousand people were reading posts about the climate strike on social media platforms.

Swedish high school student Mayson Persson, fifteen, says she joined Thunberg at Parliament House the morning after she first read about the climate strike on social media. "I was there at her side," Persson says. "I have, for a few years, had an interest in the climate and have chosen to not travel by airplane or eat meat in order to lessen my impact on the climate. I joined Greta because youths are strong but we are even stronger together."[15]

Fridays for Future

Thunberg's strike for climate change was now national news in Sweden. Finally, the September 9 elections arrived and Swedes went to the polls. Thunberg and the others who had joined her in the protest were disheartened that few candidates for the Swedish parliament talked about climate change as they campaigned for office. Thunberg's original plan was to return to school following the election, but by now she realized her mission to raise awareness about climate change was just beginning. Thunberg did return to school, but going forward she vowed to skip school every Friday to carry on her protest against climate change. Thunberg decided to call the new phase of the campaign "Fridays for Future."

> "I joined Greta because youths are strong but we are even stronger together."[15]
>
> —Mayson Persson, fifteen-year-old Swedish high school student

The message soon spread across Sweden. Now, thousands of Swedish students were joining her by skipping school every Friday. By the end of the year, the message spread to other European nations as well. Tens of thousands of school students from numerous European countries started skipping school on Fridays to protest the failure of their governments to address climate change. And they were doing more than just staying home from school. The students met in front of governmental buildings in their capital cities to rally and demand action by their countries' lawmakers to address the emission of greenhouse gases into the atmosphere.

In January 2019, Fridays for Future rallies drew one hundred thousand young people in Brussels, Belgium, and eighty thousand in Paris, France. "We come here with the right intentions, to protest in peace and to raise awareness about climate change, because we want to be on the right side of history," said nineteen-year-old Elisa Kiambi at a rally in Brussels. "It is time for the government to act."[16] Meanwhile, in Berlin, Germany, ten thousand young people braved winter temperatures to rally in front of the government headquarters of the Ministry of Economics and Technology. The ministry helps set national policy in Germany on the amount of pollutants that industries are permitted to release into the atmosphere. "We tell people, dress warmly, because we are only getting started,"[17] said Luisa Neubauer, a twenty-two-year-old university student who helped organize the protests in Berlin.

> "We come here with the right intentions, to protest in peace and to raise awareness about climate change, because we want to be on the right side of history."[16]
>
> —Elisa Kiambi, nineteen-year-old participant at a climate rally in Brussels, Belgium

The Extinction Rebellion

While the Fridays for Future strikes were being staged across Europe, Thunberg found herself very much in demand to appear at the rallies and address the huge crowds. On October 31, 2018, she was invited to speak at a rally in London, England, organized by an activist environmental group known as Extinction Rebellion.

The Thunbergs went to London as a family, driving in an electric car they had purchased. Electric cars are powered by batteries and electric motors, not gasoline-burning internal combustion engines, and therefore the vehicles do not emit carbon dioxide pollution. The drive took eight hours from Stockholm to the city of Calais, France. There the Thunbergs boarded a train that traveled the rest of the way to London through the Chunnel, the 31-mile (50 km) tunnel beneath the English Channel that connects France and Great Britain. The train ride took another two hours. If

In January 2019 Thunberg gave an address at the World Economic Forum in Davos, Switzerland. She spoke about how old methods of producing energy (burning coal, oil, and natural gas) have resulted in high greenhouse gas emissions.

the Thunbergs had chosen to fly from Stockholm to London, the flight would have taken less than three hours. But jetliners emit carbon dioxide pollution, and the Thunbergs had decided they would no longer contribute to climate change.

Arriving in London, Thunberg found herself facing a crowd of one thousand protesters in the city's Parliament Square. She told the protesters that she first learned about climate change as a young girl. She said,

I remember thinking that it was very strange, that humans who are an animal species among others, could be capable of changing the earth's climate. Because, if we were and if it was really happening, we wouldn't be talking about anything else. As soon as you turned on the TV, everything would be about that. Headlines, radio, newspapers. You would never read or hear about anything else. As if there was a world war going on.

But no one ever talked about it. Ever. If burning fossil fuels was so bad, that it threatened our very existence, how could we just continue like before? Why were there no restrictions? Why wasn't it made illegal? To me, that did not add up. It was too unreal.[18]

Waiting Is Not an Option

Six weeks after the Extinction Rebellion rally, Thunberg was invited to address a much different type of group. Meeting in Katowice, Poland, in December 2018, organizers of the UN Climate Change Conference asked her to speak before the delegates. The conference is an annual meeting of UN officials and others tasked with assessing the progress nations have made in stemming the rise of climate change.

An invitation to speak before a UN body provided Thunberg with an audience composed not of protesting school students but of government leaders. The Thunbergs drove their electric car from Stockholm to Katowice—a distance of 628 miles (1,010 km)—in order to avoid flying in a commercial jetliner. When the Thunbergs arrived, they were welcomed by Polish students who had walked out of their classes to personally greet Greta. "Adults sometimes forget about the young people,"[19] said Małgorzata Czachowska, one of the Polish students who was there.

Many of the students held signs that said "12 Years Left," a reference to a 2018 study that had been released by the UN Intergovernmental Panel on Climate Change. That study stated that leaders of government and industry must make substantial changes in reducing greenhouse gas emissions by 2030 or else the effects of climate change would not be reversible.

Greta Thunberg and the Electric Car

Electric cars are powered by batteries. Unlike vehicles powered by gasoline, electric cars do not emit carbon dioxide. But although most auto manufacturers offer electric vehicles for sale, they are still rarely seen on streets and highways. Statistics released in 2019 by the US Energy Information Administration show that electric vehicles comprise just 2.1 percent of global auto sales.

Greta Thunberg's parents purchased an electric car so they could drive her to climate activism events throughout Europe. And when Thunberg arrived in America in August 2019 to speak before the United Nations and other organizations, film star and former California governor Arnold Schwarzenegger provided Thunberg with an electric car so she could attend events throughout the US.

Thunberg is not alone in her desire to go by electric vehicle only. Insiders in the motor vehicle industry report that it is becoming harder to sell gasoline-powered vehicles to young people. "Everyone I know under 25 isn't the slightest bit interested in cars," says Jeremy Clarkson, host of the British car-themed television series *The Grand Tour*. "Greta Thunberg has killed the car show. They're taught at school, before they say 'Mummy and Daddy,' that cars are evil, and it's in their heads."

Quoted in Colin Beresford, "Activist Greta Thunberg Wins Accolades, Insults for Promoting EVs," *Car and Driver*, December 11, 2019. www.caranddriver.com.

Invited to Davos

During the Katowice meeting, Thunberg scolded the UN delegates for not taking definitive action to stem the emission of greenhouse gases. "You are not mature enough to tell it like is," she said at the UN meeting. "Even that burden you leave to us children. But I don't care about being popular. I care about climate justice and the living planet."[20]

A few weeks after the Katowice meeting, yet another group of influential leaders invited Thunberg to address their meeting. This time, the invitation came from the World Economic Forum

(WEF), an international organization composed of business leaders, political leaders, diplomats, and others. Each year, members convene for a convention in Davos, Switzerland, to discuss and adopt policies they hope will bolster the economies of nations and improve quality of life worldwide. But many environmentalists contend that in their efforts to accomplish these goals, international industries have relied on old methods of producing energy: burning oil, coal, and natural gas, which have resulted in high greenhouse gas emissions.

That was the message Thunberg delivered to the delegates at the January 2019 conference in Davos. Arriving at the Swiss village by electric train, Thunberg challenged the delegates to start doing business with the goal of preserving the climate. "Our house is on fire," she told them. "At Davos, people like to talk about success, but financial success has come with a price tag, and on the climate we have failed. And unless we recognize the failures of our system, there will be unspoken suffering."[21]

Protests Spread to America

Thunberg's speeches before the UN Climate Change Conference, the WEF, and the Extinction Rebellion rally made headlines across Europe. Young people throughout the European countries were taking up the cause. Thousands of students were skipping school on Fridays to attend rallies and demand action on climate change. By early 2019, Thunberg's message had also spread across the Atlantic Ocean.

In New York City, students began staging their own protests. Seventh-grade student Alexandria Villaseñor, thirteen, began a Fridays for Future protest at the UN headquarters. She carried a picket sign that called for action on climate change. Each Friday, well into 2019, Villaseñor stood firm, protest sign in hand, regardless of the weather outside UN headquarters. "I am too young to vote and to lobby," she told a reporter. "But I can sit down with a sign and make my voice heard."[22] Meanwhile, across the city, another New York student, ten-year-old Zayne Cowie, staged his own Fridays for Future protests at New York City Hall. Cowie was accompanied during his protests by his mother, New York City artist Eva Mosher. "Being there with him made me realize that this is much

> "I am too young to vote and to lobby. But I can sit down with a sign and make my voice heard."[22]
>
> —Alexandria Villaseñor, thirteen-year-old climate protester from New York City

more urgent," Mosher said. "It was time to get way more serious about this—to start looking at actual self-sacrifice as a way to make things happen."[23]

And across the country, twelve-year-old Haven Coleman carried out her Fridays for Future protests in Denver, Colorado. Coleman carried her "School Strike for Climate" sign before numerous governmental buildings in the Colorado capital. "Once I learned about climate change, I was like, 'Oh my gosh, this is affecting me, it's affecting the whole world, it's affecting so many people in that it's been ruling my life and it will be ruling my life for my whole life.' And so, I was like, 'I gotta do something,'"[24] Coleman told a reporter.

At first, the protests staged by Villaseñor, Cowie, and Coleman were solitary vigils, but soon American students rallied in large numbers as well. On March 15, 2019, a worldwide strike by student activists was staged. An estimated 1.6 million people in 133 countries took part in the strike, including tens of thousands of American students who skipped school that day in major cities, suburban communities, and small towns across the country.

Many of the students said they joined the protest because they fear for their futures. "It's not going to affect a lot of the people who are in politics right now, who are old and own companies, and who are rich enough to support themselves. It affects us, the kids, who are in school right now, who can't vote, who don't have a voice,"[25] said thirteen-year-old Harper Alderson during a protest in front of New York City Hall.

Voyage of the *Malizia II*

By the summer of 2019, it was clear the student protests were re-igniting interest in government officials to address climate change. The UN announced that it would convene a new conference to address climate change, scheduling the Climate Action Summit for September 21 through September 23 at UN headquarters in New York. As evidence that the student protests were gaining traction among the delegates, UN officials announced that they had invited Thunberg to address the summit. Thunberg immediately accepted.

On August 14, Thunberg and her father arrived in the British seaside community of Plymouth to board the *Malizia II*, a sailboat that would make the trek across the Atlantic Ocean to New York City. The sailboat and its crew were made available to the Thunbergs without charge by its owner, Boris Herrmann, a noted German yacht racer who served as skipper for the voyage.

The voyage from Plymouth to New York ultimately took fifteen days. A flight from London to New York City would have taken about eight hours, but—as with their prior trips to London, Katowice, and Davos—the Thunbergs were committed to making the trip without contributing to carbon dioxide emissions. The *Malizia II* relied on the prevailing winds to propel it across the Atlantic. All the appliances on board—kitchen equipment, communications devices, and other machines—were powered by batteries as well as solar panels affixed to the cabin roof.

Thunberg spent much of the journey in her cabin, writing in her journal. She also communicated with the thousands of supporters who were following the journey through social media. Soon after the voyage commenced, Thunberg reported that the seas were rough and she was enduring long spells of nausea—but planned to see the journey through to the end. "I feel a bit seasick and it's not going to be comfortable but that I can live with," Thunberg wrote on a Facebook post. "If it's really hard then I just have to think it's only for two weeks."[26]

CLIMATE ACTION SUMMIT 2019

In September 2019 Thunberg spoke at the United Nations headquarters before the delegates to the Climate Action Summit. As she had done before, she scolded the delegates for failing to take necessary action to cut back on greenhouse gas emissions.

No Longer Ignored

On August 14, the *Malizia II* arrived in New York Harbor. Hundreds of climate activists were waiting. They cheered as Thunberg stepped off the sailboat. Many of those in attendance were young people who broke into chants, "Sea levels are rising and so are we!" and "There is no Planet B!"[27]

Starting on September 20, the day before the UN Climate Action Summit was set to convene in New York City, climate activists staged a weeklong series of protests. Some twenty-five hundred events in 163 countries were staged. More than 4 million protesters participated. In New York City, for example, some sixty thousand protesters staged a demonstration in Foley Square outside New York City Hall. At the end of the rally, Thunberg ascended a stage to address the protesters. She issued a warning to the UN delegates, whom she was scheduled to address. "Change is coming whether they like it or not," she said. "Do you think they hear us?"[28]

Nominated for the Nobel Peace Prize

The Nobel Peace Prize is an honor given to an individual or group that works to promote world peace. The prize was established by the will of Swedish inventor Alfred Nobel more than a century ago. Over the years, diplomats, presidents, and other world leaders have earned the honor. In 2019, Greta Thunberg was nominated for the Nobel Peace Prize by three members of the Norwegian parliament. "We have proposed Greta Thunberg because if we do nothing to halt climate change, it will be the cause of wars, conflict and refugees," said Freddy Andre Ovstegard, one of the Norwegian lawmakers who nominated Thunberg. "Greta Thunberg has launched a mass movement which I see as a major contribution to peace."

The prize is awarded by the Norwegian Nobel Committee, which is appointed by the Norwegian parliament. Ultimately, the Nobel Committee did not select Thunberg for the prize, selecting instead Abiy Ahmed Ali, the prime minister of Ethiopia who was instrumental in ending a twenty-year civil war in his nation.

Although climate activists, among them former US vice president Al Gore, have won the Nobel Peace Prize in the past, observers suggested that the current members of the Nobel Committee wish to hew more closely to the wishes of Alfred Nobel, who directed the prize to be awarded for efforts to end armed conflicts.

Quoted in BBC, "Greta Thunberg Nominated for Nobel Peace Prize for Climate Activism," March 14, 2019, www.bbc.com.

Finally, on September 23, Thunberg arrived at the UN headquarters and spoke before the delegates to the Climate Action Summit. As she did at the earlier UN meeting in Katowice, she scolded the delegates for failing to take action to stem the emission of greenhouse gases. She told the delegates, "You have stolen my dreams and my childhood with your empty words. And yet I'm one of the lucky ones. People are suffering. People are dying. Entire ecosystems are collapsing. We are in the beginning of a mass extinction, and all you can talk about is money and fairy tales of eternal economic growth. How dare you!"[29]

Thunberg's speech before the UN Climate Action Summit made international news and sparked further demonstrations across the globe. Just thirteen months earlier, the young school-girl had maintained a solitary vigil in Stockholm, sitting on a hard cobblestone sidewalk, her protest sign propped up next to her, as she implored members of the Swedish parliament to take action against climate change. She was largely ignored that first day but now, after millions of young people had rallied behind her, there would be no more ignoring Thunberg or what she had to say about the future of the earth.

Chapter Three

Standing Up to the Climate Change Deniers

In the decades since NASA scientist James E. Hansen first warned the US Senate about the effect of greenhouse gases, more and more Americans have come to realize that climate change is a threat to the future of the planet. But some Americans as well as citizens of other nations have been steadfast in their beliefs that the earth's climate is not warming. Meanwhile, some people who acknowledge the earth's climate is warming do not believe it is due to the emissions of greenhouse gases into the atmosphere. In other words, they do not believe humans are the cause of climate change.

One of the most outspoken climate change deniers is James Inhofe, US senator from Oklahoma. Inhofe is a former chairman of the Senate Committee on Environment and Public Works—a legislative panel charged with writing America's environmental protection laws. In a 2003 speech on the Senate floor, shortly after assuming chairmanship of the Environmental and Public Works Committee, Inhofe said,

Anyone who pays even cursory attention to the issue understands that scientists vigorously disagree over whether human activities are responsible for global warming or whether those activities will precipitate national disasters. Only the scaremongers agree. I submit, furthermore, that not only is there a debate but the debate is shifting away from those who subscribe to global-warming alarmism. After studying the issue over the last several years, I believe the balance of the evidence offers strong proof that natural variability, not manmade, is the overwhelming factor influencing climate, and that manmade gases are virtually irrelevant.[30]

Inhofe and other climate change deniers represent a minority of Americans and citizens of other countries. A 2019 CBS News poll reported that just 9 percent of Americans do not believe the climate is warming. Moreover, 29 percent of the respondents who did acknowledge the earth's climate is warming do not believe burning fossil fuels is the cause. Rather, they insist the warming climate is due to natural factors.

But even though climate change deniers and skeptics are in the minority, they often speak with very loud voices. And as Greta Thunberg found herself rising to international prominence in her call for climate activism, their voices were often directed, quite angrily, at the teenager from Sweden.

> "Anyone who pays even cursory attention to the issue understands that scientists vigorously disagree over whether human activities are responsible for global warming."[30]
>
> —US senator James Inhofe of Oklahoma

Criticized on Fox News

One of the first critics to denounce Thunberg and her call for activism was Marc Morano, a former member of Inhofe's Senate staff. After leaving Inhofe's staff, Morano went to work for the Washington, DC–based group Committee for a Constructive Tomorrow, or CFACT. The group's primary mission is to offer arguments against acceptance of the science of climate change. Morano heads CFACT's website, www.ClimateDepot.com. Appearing on the Fox News show *Fox & Friends* the same day Thunberg addressed the UN Climate Action Summit in New York, Morano said, "She sells fear. Greta Thunberg started in Sweden every Friday outside the Swedish parliament and it spread—to skip school in order to have a future. In other words, she's actually said, 'Why should kids go to school if they have a future that will be no more unless government passes [environmental protection] laws."[31]

Ainsley Earhardt, one of the show's hosts, agreed with Morano. Earhardt suggested many of the young people who were participating in the school strikes and climate rallies were doing so because of peer pressure. "If you really want to protest, do something challenging," Morano added. "Why would you skip school? That's an easy thing for any kid to do."[32]

Criticisms leveled at Thunberg on Fox News continued. A day after Thunberg made her speech before the UN Climate Action Summit, political commentator Michael Knowles appeared on a

James Inhofe (pictured), a US senator from Oklahoma, is one of the most outspoken opponents of the idea that humans cause climate change.

Fox News broadcast. "If it were about science it would be led by scientists rather than by politicians and a mentally ill Swedish child who is being exploited by her parents,"[33] Knowles said, in an apparent reference to Thunberg's Asperger's syndrome.

"If it were about science it would be led by scientists rather than by politicians and a mentally ill Swedish child who is being exploited by her parents."[33]

—Conservative commentator Michael Knowles

The blowback against Knowles and Fox News was immediate. Appearing with Knowles on the broadcast was commentator Christopher Hahn, who supports climate activism. "How dare you?" Hahn said, as Knowles finished his remarks. "You're a grown man and you're attacking a child. Shame on you. . . . Maybe on your podcast you get away and say whatever you want because nobody's listening. You're on national television. Be a grown-up when you're talking about children."[34]

Ultimately, Fox News issued an apology to Thunberg, calling Knowles' comments inappropriate. The network said it would no longer schedule Knowles as a guest on its news and talk shows. "The comment made by Michael Knowles who was a guest . . . tonight was disgraceful," a spokesperson for Fox News said. "We apologize to Greta Thunberg and to our viewers."[35]

Why Many Conservatives Oppose New Climate Laws

But kicking Knowles off its broadcasts did not mean other commentators on Fox News ceased their criticism of Thunberg. Appearing on her nightly Fox News broadcast the evening after Thunberg's speech to the UN, commentator Laura Ingraham showed a brief video of the Swedish activist's speech, then said, "Cede control of our economy, our way of life, our way of transport, how many children you want to have, and if we don't go along, we will be punished by our own children. Does anyone else find that chilling?"[36]

As the comments of Morano, Earhardt, Knowles, and Ingraham illustrate, Fox News is a well-known outlet for conservative voices in America. Political conservatives generally support as little

While many political conservatives and business leaders were vocal in their criticisms of Greta Thunberg, one group that managed to keep its complaints out of the media included leaders of many well-established environmental groups. Numerous organizations had spent decades warning of the dangers of climate change and backing candidates for public office who shared their views. Many groups have financed scientific studies of the effects on greenhouse gas emissions. And yet, to many environmental activists, all their efforts seemed to go unnoticed until a sixteen-year-old girl from Stockholm started skipping school and speaking her mind.

When *Time* magazine selected Thunberg as its Person of the Year, the publication's reporters tracked down the leaders of international environmental groups to find out whether they did, in fact, harbor a degree of resentment toward Thunberg. "On the record, no major environmental group would say anything remotely negative," the magazine reported.

Nevertheless, Rachel Kyte, the dean of the international affairs school at Tufts University in Massachusetts, confirmed to *Time* that leaders of some well-known environmental groups felt that when Thunberg entered the world stage, their longtime efforts to reverse climate change had not received the recognition they felt they deserved. Said Kyte, herself a longtime environmental activist, "They want the needle moved, too. They just want to be the ones that get the credit for moving it."

Quoted in Charlotte Alter, Susan Haynes, and Justin Worland, "The Conscience," *Time*, December 23–30, 2019, p. 62.

governmental intervention as possible in people's lives. Therefore, many conservatives oppose new laws for a variety of issues, including addressing climate change. While many conservatives may endorse climate science, they believe the answers to reversing climate change should come out of private enterprise—not out of new laws adopted by governments. In other words, instead of seeing governments mandate that fields of solar panels replace coal-fired power plants to produce electricity, conservatives would prefer to see private companies establish solar panel fields on their own without government intervention. And so as Thunberg called for the governments of the world to take action to stem the emission of greenhouse gases, Fox News provided a forum for conservatives to oppose her activism.

Criticism against Thunberg and her cause emerged from other conservative outlets as well. Writing for the magazine *American Conservative*—in an opinion column headlined "By All Means, Let's Criticize Greta Thunberg"—commentator Bill Wirtz took aim at the Swedish teen. He wrote,

> People are to be burdened with higher energy prices and more expensive air travel, while the engines in their cars are gradually made illegal. Does Greta care? Probably not—she is more than willing to throw the prosperity of future generations under the bus. She asks those she may never encounter to make enormous sacrifices, lose their jobs, see their families abroad less often, see their children less after doubling their commutes to and from work, not allowing themselves to enjoy steak. Those who have worked all their lives to carve out a future for themselves and their children, who built a free and prosperous world, are demonized as backwards and willfully mischievous. Yet when they, after all this ill-informed hysteria, make jokes or dare to criticize Greta, they're castigated and sacrificed on the altar of media shaming.[37]

Thunberg did not keep silent as she was slammed by the conservative media. Following her speech before the UN, Thunberg and her father returned to the *Malizia II* for the return trip to Plymouth, England. News reporters met the Thunbergs at the dock in New York City and asked Greta to respond to the criticism from the conservative commentators. She said, "If they are attacking me, then that means they have no argument to speak of and their debate only involves attacking me. That means we've already won. We have become the bad guys who have to tell people these uncomfortable things because no one else wants to, or dares to."[38]

The Corporate World Speaks Up

Many companies in the United States and elsewhere have adopted business practices that help sustain the environment. The giant retailer Walmart intends to eventually power all its stores through solar energy; computer maker Dell now accepts all its old computers back from owners free of charge so that the company can recycle the old machines; and Nike, the manufacturer of athletic shoes, now uses mostly recycled materials in its products. Still, many business leaders agree with the conservative viewpoint that government should stay out of their business. As demands from Thunberg and other environmental activists for laws to reverse greenhouse gas emissions have grown over the years, many business leaders have staunchly resisted. They have argued that forcing them to give up reliance on fossil fuels would adversely affect their companies and, ultimately, their profits. In other words, they fear that addressing climate change would cost too much money. And so they have used their financial muscle to support political candidates who agree with their positions on relying on fossil fuels to make their factories run, power their delivery trucks, and fly their goods to domestic and foreign markets.

> "If they are attacking me, then that means they have no argument to speak of and their debate only involves attacking me. That means we've already won."[38]
>
> —Greta Thunberg

Their support for politicians who agree with their positions may help explain how a climate change denier like Senator Inhofe was able to ascend to head an important legislative committee charged with writing laws to protect the environment. (Inhofe stepped down as chairman of the committee in 2017, but as of 2020 he continued to serve as a member of the panel.) Inhofe's

Because the airline industry is a huge contributor to carbon dioxide in the atmosphere, Thunberg has spoken out against it and given up air travel. She has been criticized by airline industry executives for her outspoken views about their role in climate change.

home state of Oklahoma is home to a robust oil and natural gas drilling industry that is vital to his state's economy. More than fifty thousand Oklahomans work in the oil and gas production industry. When Inhofe was last re-elected to the Senate in 2014, he won with 68 percent of the vote. According to the political watchdog group OpenSecrets.org, officials in the oil and gas industries have contributed more than $2 million to Inhofe's campaign committee since 1989. And so, as Thunberg's call for climate activism grew, she found many of her staunchest critics were executives of some of the world's largest corporations and the politicians they helped put in office.

One such critic is Bernard Arnault, chairman of LVMH, a French corporation that manufactures and distributes luxury goods, such as jewelry, expensive wines, fashions, and furs. Arnault, a billionaire, is considered to be France's richest citizen. Two days after Thunberg's speech to the UN, Arnault complained that LVMH had already taken steps to reduce its reliance on fossil fuels and would, going forward, continue to look for ways to use clean energy, such

Naomi Seibt: The Anti-Greta

Just as climate change activists have found a young hero in Greta Thunberg, climate change deniers have found their own young hero. It is Naomi Seibt, a nineteen-year-old YouTube star from Münster, Germany. In 2019 Seibt, started posting videos on YouTube questioning climate science and insisting that global warming is a hoax. She soon came to the attention of conservative groups which promoted her as the true voice of young people on the issue of climate change. Some conservatives are calling her the *anti-Greta*.

"Today climate change science really is not science at all," says Seibt. "The goal [of climate scientists] is to shame humanity. Climate change alarmism at its very core is a despicably antihuman ideology and we are told to look down at our achievements with guilt, with shame and disgust, and not even to take into account the many major benefits we have achieved by using fossil fuels as our main energy source."

Seibt's YouTube channel reported some 77,000 subscribers in 2020. Her campaign to promote climate change denial has been funded by the Heartland Institute, an Illinois-based group that backs conservative policies. The organization finances Seibt's travel to give speeches to conservative groups as well as the production costs for her YouTube videos. Says the Heartland Institute: "Naomi will be working on communicating the climate realism message to her generation—which has marinated in apocalyptic nonsense their whole lives—for audiences in both in Europe and the United States."

Quoted in Stephanie Kirchgaessner and Emily Holden, "Naomi Seibt: 'Anti-Greta' Activist Called White Nationalist an Inspiration." *The Guardian*, February 28, 2020. www.theguardian.com.

Heartland Institute, "Youtube Personality Naomi Seibt Joins the Heartland Institute," February 11, 2020. www.heartland .org.

as solar and wind power, to make and sell its goods. But he worried that government mandates would adversely affect LVMH's business. "If we don't want to go backwards, we still need growth," he maintained. As for Thunberg, Arnault said, "She's a dynamic young girl, but she's surrendering completely to catastrophism. I find that her views are demoralizing for young people."[39]

Airlines Fear an Air Travel Ban

Other business leaders joined Arnault in their criticisms of Thunberg. Among them were executives in the airline industry. Thunberg had, of course, given up air travel because of the massive amounts of oil-based fuel it takes to propel a jetliner. A UN study found that air travel is responsible for producing some 992 million tons (900 million metric tons) of carbon dioxide emissions per year. Moreover, the study predicted that unless alternatives are found, that number is likely to triple by 2050. Said Brandon Glover, the UN official who headed the study, "The climate challenge for aviation is worse than anyone expected."[40]

The study was released days after Thunberg stepped off the *Malizia II* in New York Harbor to deliver her speech to the UN Climate Action Summit. Its effect could already be seen in Europe. Environmental activists in Germany, for instance, called on their government to ban air travel in that nation in favor of ground transportation methods that would rely on electric cars and trains.

Amid this mounting pressure, airline executives singled out Thunberg for criticism. One airline industry leader, Alexandre de Juniac, complained about what he regarded as an anti–air travel movement that Thunberg appeared to be spearheading. De Juniac is head of the International Air Transport Association, a trade association representing nearly three hundred of the world's airlines. De Juniac has admitted in news interviews that he is unconvinced that carbon emissions are the cause of climate change. He believes Thunberg has wrongly blamed air travelers and airlines as primarily responsible for carbon emissions. "We are not the only polluter on this planet, and we have taken [on] the subject . . . directly and massively," he told reporters. He added that Thunberg should understand that the airline industry is searching for alternatives to oil-based jet fuel. "I would like to tell her that what we are targeting is to fly more and pollute less,"[41] he said.

Speaking in Thunberg's defense, Andrew Murphy, a spokesperson for the Brussels, Belgium–based environmental advocacy group Transport & Environment, said it has long been clear that the airline industry is a major polluter. He pointed out that by 2020, airplanes powered by solar energy or battery power were still very much in the experimental phase. He said, "Monsieur de Juniac doesn't like hearing the hard truths from Mademoiselle Thunberg, but aviation emissions are soaring and electric aircraft are decades away."[42]

Bolsonaro's Stinging Criticism

While corporate executives and conservative commentators took aim at Thunberg, perhaps the most severe criticism was leveled at the young activist by the leaders of national governments. These are the very people Thunberg and her followers hoped to persuade to adopt measures to stem the release of greenhouse gases. Many of these national leaders were elected by conservative voters, which helps explain why they were so dismissive of Thunberg's campaign. In Brazil, for example, President Jair Bolsonaro told reporters, "It's amazing how much space the press gives this kind of *pirralha*." In Portuguese, the native language of Brazil, the word *pirralha* translates as "little brat."[43] Bolsonaro is an ardent conservative and climate change denier.

> "Monsieur de Juniac doesn't like hearing the hard truths from Mademoiselle Thunberg, but aviation emissions are soaring and electric aircraft are decades away."[42]
>
> —Belgian climate activist Andrew Murphy

In 2019 Brazil experienced some of the worst wildfires in that country's history. The National Institute for Space Research, an agency of the Brazilian government, reported that raging wildfires had destroyed 3,769 square miles (9,760 square km) of the nation's Amazon rain forest. Climate scientists worldwide say that climate change is at least partly to blame for these and other wildfires.

Out-of-control wildfires have also plagued Australia. In late 2019 and early 2020, fires swept across that continent, engulfing some 28,000 square miles (73,000 square km) of land. Some sixteen hundred homes were destroyed. In December 2019, as the

Disastrous wildfires plagued Australia in late 2019 and early 2020. Thunberg has openly criticized the Australian government for not doing enough to curb greenhouse gas emissions even after facing the catastrophic wildfires.

fires raged across Australia, Thunberg criticized the Australian government for doing little to curb greenhouse gas emissions. "Not even catastrophes like these seem to bring any political action," Thunberg posted on her Twitter account. "How is this possible? Because we still fail to make the connection between the climate crisis and increased extreme weather events and nature disasters like the Australia fires. That's what has to change."[44]

Scott Morrison, the conservative Australian prime minister who maintains that the coal mining industry is vital to his country's economy, fired back at Thunberg. Although not mentioning the Swedish teen by name, it was clear whom he was talking about when he told reporters: "We'll do in Australia what we think is right for Australia. . . . I'm not here to try and impress people overseas. I'm here to do the right job for Australians and put them first."[45]

Taking on Trump

Perhaps the most stinging criticism of Thunberg by a national leader was leveled by US president Donald Trump, also a political conservative. In fact, Trump has declared he does not believe the earth's climate is changing. Shortly after *Time* selected Thunberg as its Person of the Year, Trump wrote on his Twitter account that he didn't think the Swedish teenager merited the honor. "So ridiculous," Trump wrote to his 71 million followers on Twitter. "Greta must work on her Anger Management problem, then go to a good old fashioned movie with a friend! Chill Greta, Chill!"[46]

Trump and Thunberg had actually nearly crossed paths on September 23, 2019, the day she addressed the UN Climate Action Summit. They stood a few feet apart from one another as Thunberg approached the stage, but the two did not meet. After Trump criticized her on Twitter, Thunberg recalled that occasion, telling reporters she was happy that she had not had the opportunity to speak with Trump. "I don't think I would have said anything because he's obviously not listening to scientists and experts, why would he listen to me? I probably wouldn't have said anything, wouldn't have wasted my time,"[47] she said.

As for the attacks leveled at her by Bolsonaro, Morrison, and Trump, Thunberg said, "Those attacks are just funny. It means they are terrified of young people bringing change, which they don't want, but that is just a proof that we are actually doing something and they see us as some kind of threat."[48]

It had now been just a little more than a year since Thunberg started her school strike for the climate. In that time, the campaign had grown from a lonely vigil in front of Sweden's Parliament House to a worldwide campaign supported by millions of climate activists. Perhaps, there was now no better evidence that her campaign was working than the fact that the world's climate change deniers were expressing criticism of the campaign. It seemed that their carbon-friendly policies were now very much threatened by Thunberg and her followers.

Chapter Four

The Greta Effect

By early 2020, Greta Thunberg's refusal to travel by air had earned a name of its own in popular culture: *flygskam*. Pronounced "fleeg-skaam," it is a Swedish term that translates into English as "flight-shame." In other words, more and more travelers were taking part in *flygskam*—placing blame on the international airline industry for contributing to climate change. And they were doing so by either electing not to travel at all or instead finding other ways to reach their destinations, such as booking seats on trains. "It does seem like a switch has flipped," says Seth Kaplan, a journalist who covers the airline industry. "For a while, there was this very incremental recognition of the urgency (of climate change), and then over the past year or so all this has really gotten into the spotlight—aided by Greta Thunberg."[49] Evidence of *flygskam*'s effect on the Swedish airline industry could be seen in ticket sales for train travel. In 2018 Sweden's national railway reported that it had sold about 1.5 million more tickets than it sold the year before.

Many airline executives noted that the number of occupied seats on their routes had dropped throughout 2018 and 2019—the period in which Thunberg's activism grew in international prominence. Rickard Gustafson, the chief executive officer of Scandinavian Airlines, Sweden's largest air carrier, acknowledged in 2019 that his airline's business had declined by 2 percent over the previous year. He blamed the *flygskam* movement and added that the airline industry must find a way to produce airliners that do not contribute to greenhouse gas emissions. "The journey toward a fossil-free footprint will be long, but I'm a technology optimist," Gustafson said. "One day a scientist will figure out how to replace the current jet engine, and I think those planes will become available to all of us in, say, 20 years' time."[50]

Other airlines saw similar drops in ticket sales as a result of *flygskam*. In Germany, officials reported that domestic flights—flights from one German city to another—had fallen by 12 percent in 2019. Meanwhile, a 2019 poll commissioned by the Swiss bank UBS asked six thousand people to discuss how they choose modes of travel. The poll revealed that one in five travelers in the United States, France, Great Britain, and Germany had cut air travel by at least one flight in the past year because of climate concerns. In France, Anne Rigail, the chief executive officer of Air France, the country's national airline, said the *flygskam* movement is definitely to blame for the drop off in air travel. Said Rigail, "I think it's our biggest challenge."[51]

Carbon Offsets

Flygskam is only one element of what is now known as the Greta Effect: a trend, inspired by Thunberg, to hold greenhouse gas emitters accountable for climate change. Climate activists and their supporters may do so by participating in the *flygskam* movement—refusing to fly—or by participating in a number of other strategies to curb greenhouse gas emissions.

One of the strategies attributed to the Greta Effect is the growth in the number of individuals and corporations worldwide that have agreed to invest in so-called carbon offsets. Typically, environmental groups raise money from individuals, foundations, and corporations to finance projects that provide energy to impoverished communities without the need to rely on fossil fuels. Donors may continue to burn fossil fuels for their own needs, but their dollars are helping to offset greenhouse gas emissions elsewhere.

One such group that raises money to fund carbon offsets is the Somerset, England–based Climate Stewards. In late 2019 David Hughes, chairperson of Climate Stewards, reported, "The whole business of carbon offsetting has suddenly taken off. It has been so gratifying to see a lot of individuals choosing to offset over the last 12 months—the numbers have more than doubled. We are seeing the Greta Effect, the impact of Extinction Rebellion . . . the school strikes, all of these coming together."[52]

Financial donations to Climate Stewards increased by more than 150 percent between 2018 and 2019. The growth seen by

Because of the international airline industry's contribution to climate change, some people have followed Thunberg's lead and opted to either not travel at all, or book seats on trains and travel by rail.

Climate Stewards is not unique. The Hong Kong–based organization Green Queen Media, which covers environmental news worldwide, reported in late 2019,

> Inspired by Greta Thunberg, who has raised the attention of our planet's ecological crisis, organizations involved in carbon offsetting have seen as much as a four-fold increase in support for carbon mitigation over the past 18 months. Carbon offsetting projects include all transformative projects that reduce emissions in developing countries, such as providing [non-carbon-emitting] stoves in kitchens, improving access to clean water to reduce greenhouse gases generated from burning firewood to boil water, and forest restoration projects."[53]

Forest restoration—the planting of new trees—is regarded as a carbon offset project because trees help to scrub the atmosphere by absorbing carbon dioxide gas.

Green Queen Media went on to report that Climate Care, a private company based in Oxford, England, that helps individuals and businesses implement carbon-offset projects, estimated that its efforts had offset the emission of some 22 million tons (20 million metric tons) of greenhouse gases in 2019. In 2018—the year in which Thunberg's climate activism started to grow in prominence—Climate Care's projects had resulted in a carbon offset of just 2.2 million tons (2 million metric tons).

Young Activists Rise Up

These efforts to reduce greenhouse gas emissions are mostly being carried out by young people. But many young climate activists think they can accomplish more than just refusing to fly or donating to carbon offset projects. By 2020, many young people were starting their own climate activist groups and were developing their own strategies to call attention to the climate crisis.

Alexandria Villaseñor, the thirteen-year-old New York City student who started her own Fridays for Future protests in 2019, eventually went on to start a climate activism group: Earth Uprising. By 2020, Earth Uprising had evolved into an international organization of climate activists who plan and organize their own demonstrations. "It's very sad that the weight of the climate crisis has been put on my generation's shoulders—that we have to organize and mobilize in order to have a future," Villaseñor says. "We're finding more ways to take direct action and get attention from adults. It's really upsetting because we shouldn't have to do this in the first place."[54]

Earth Uprising was instrumental in planning the September 2019 climate strikes in America. Statistics on the number of young people who have become affiliated with Earth Uprising are not available, but the group's Twitter account boasts more than four thousand followers. Moreover, according to the group's website, its membership includes young people in more than a dozen countries, among them the United States, Sweden, Spain, Scotland, Russia, and Pakistan.

Meanwhile, Villaseñor has found herself much in demand as a speaker at international events—in much the same way that Thunberg has found her time in demand since 2018. In December 2019, Villaseñor spoke before delegates at the UN Climate Change Conference in Madrid, Spain. During the meeting, young activists in attendance interrupted the session by striding onto the stage to conduct a sit-in—a demonstration showing they would not move until world leaders took definitive action to reverse climate change. "World leaders have left us no choice,"[55] said Villaseñor.

The Green New Deal

The ranks of the young climate activists include more than just teenagers who are skipping school, joining rallies, and organizing demonstrations. Millennials are also getting involved. In the United States and other countries, millennials are becoming politically active and are running for public office—often with the commitment to address climate change.

Among the ranks of politically active millennials is Alexandria Ocasio-Cortez, who was elected to the US Congress in 2018 at the age of twenty-nine. Representing a congressional district in New York City, Ocasio-Cortez is the youngest woman ever elected to the House of Representatives.

Ocasio-Cortez and Thunberg spoke with one another in June 2019 over a video link arranged by *The Guardian*, a British newspaper. During the conversation, Ocasio-Cortez told Thunberg she was inspired by one of the Swedish teenager's speeches on the climate crisis. "I'm so excited to be having this conversation," Ocasio-Cortez told Thunberg.

I remember first hearing your speech a few months ago— I was hanging out with a friend in [New York], who said,

"Have you listened to this young woman?" And I heard your speech and was thrilled, because here in the United States, even when I was running [for office], people were saying there's no need to convey this kind of urgency [about the climate], and it's radical, and it's unnecessary. To hear you articulate the belief that I've had as well is so exciting and validating.[56]

The conversation between Ocasio-Cortez and Thunberg occurred a few months after the congresswoman introduced a measure in Congress she called the Green New Deal. The

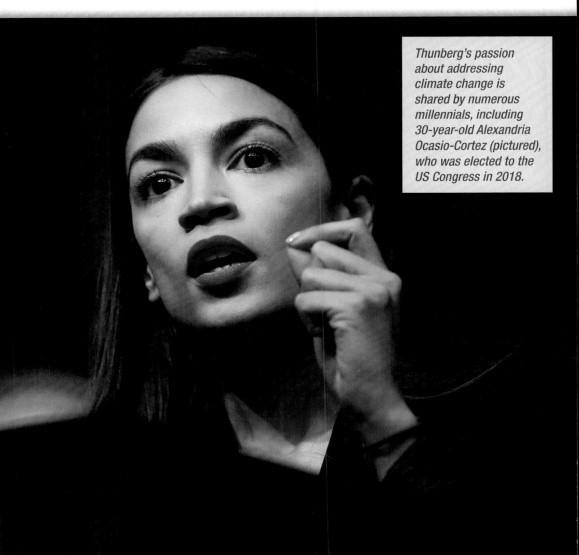

Thunberg's passion about addressing climate change is shared by numerous millennials, including 30-year-old Alexandria Ocasio-Cortez (pictured), who was elected to the US Congress in 2018.

measure is a proposed law that would take dramatic steps to reverse climate change, such as a phase out of the use of fossil fuels for all purposes—transportation, the production of electricity, and the manufacture of plastic goods and other consumer items, among others. By 2020 the measure had stalled in Congress, but many climate activists believe support is building for the law. During 2020, candidates for the Democratic nomination for US president endorsed either adoption of the Green New Deal or many of its major provisions, including a gradual conversion to renewable energy.

Sweden's Carbon Tax

Greta Thunberg has led weekly protests outside the Parliament House in Stockholm, calling on Swedish lawmakers to pass legislation that would curb greenhouse gas emissions. In fact, Sweden has long been a leader in at least one area of attacking fossil fuel use: the carbon tax.

Since 1991, the Swedish government has taxed industries that rely on fossil fuels by assessing penalties on the amount of carbon dioxide they release into the atmosphere. Sweden has the highest carbon tax among the fifteen European countries that assess the levy. Industries in Sweden pay 100 euros per metric ton of carbon dioxide they emit. (That equates to about $110 per 1.1 tons.) Swedish industries have lowered their greenhouse gas emissions by about 25 percent since the law was enacted nearly three decades ago. The high carbon tax is regarded as the main reason for this change. In Europe, the lowest carbon tax, 1 euro per metric ton, is paid by polluters in Ukraine. However, thirteen countries in Europe have no carbon tax.

America does not have a carbon tax either. Over the years, numerous members of Congress have introduced legislation proposing this tax, but the bills have died for a lack of support. One of the latest efforts occurred in 2018, when Representative Carlos Curbelo of Florida introduced a bill to tax carbon dioxide emissions. The bill remained stalled in 2020, primarily because other members of Congress oppose creating any type of new tax on US individuals or businesses.

During the conversation, Ocasio-Cortez asked Thunberg why she thinks it has fallen to young people to spearhead the climate movement. Thunberg responded,

> Many reasons, but I think the main one is that it is our future that is at risk. Most of us know that this is going to affect us in our lifetimes—it's not just something that might happen in the future. It's already here and it's going to get worse, and many of us understand that this is going to make our lives much worse. And also that as young people, we aren't as used to the system. We don't say, "It's always been like this, we can't change anything."[57]

Many national political leaders still do not seem willing to take definitive action to stem greenhouse gas emissions. But there are signs that the Greta Effect may be helping to change the minds of many people of influence. For example, in January 2020 Thunberg returned to Davos, Switzerland, to address another meeting of the World Economic Forum (WEF).

Prior to Thunberg's arrival, WEF founder Klaus Schwab said the group of business and government leaders had scheduled a number of sessions to address climate change. Many of those sessions provided details on more than 160 projects the WEF has financed to address climate change. Among those projects are helping industries implement new technologies that do not emit greenhouse gases and making the boards of directors of the world's largest corporations recognize their responsibilities for addressing carbon dioxide emissions. Also, Schwab said, members of the WEF have made a commitment to plant 1 trillion new trees worldwide. "So, if Greta comes this year, she will see that we have made substantial progress,"[58] Schwab said.

> "If Greta comes this year, she will see that we have made substantial progress."[58]
>
> —Karl Schwab, founder of the World Economic Forum

Thunberg spoke during two sessions of the WEF, and it was soon clear she did not believe the organization had gone far enough to address climate change. "Planting trees is good, of course, but it is nowhere near enough of what is needed," Thunberg told the WEF delegates. "Our house is still on fire. Your inaction is fueling the flames by the hour. And we are telling you to act as if you loved your children above all else."[59]

President's Daughter Takes Thunberg's Side

Another attendee making a return trip to Davos was President Trump. As the president's helicopter approached the landing zone in Davos, it was greeted by a message written into the snow by climate activists. The message said, "Act on Climate."

But Trump largely ignored discussions about the climate crisis during his speech to the WEF, preferring instead to talk about the health of the US economy. When asked by reporters whether he had a response to Thunberg's message to the WEF, the president responded by calling the Swedish teenager a "prophet of doom," adding that there are far bigger polluters in the world than the US. "You have another continent where the fumes are rising at levels that you can't believe. . . . I think Greta ought to focus on those places,"[60] he said. The president did not elaborate on which continent he believes adds more greenhouse gases to the atmosphere than North America.

> "You have another continent where the fumes are rising at levels that you can't believe. . . . I think Greta ought to focus on those places."[60]
>
> —US president Donald Trump

But the president's daughter, Ivanka Trump, who has served her father as an aide in the White House, said she admired Thunberg and her drive to save the climate. "I'm not going to criticize anyone who's bringing their energy and voice," Ivanka Trump told reporters. "That's not my style. I think she's elevated awareness and that's a positive thing."[61]

Thunberg attended Trump's speech before the WEF but, as she had done the year before, made no attempt to meet the US

president. Still, she would appear to have won the president's daughter over to her side, which means that at least one member of Trump's administration has found herself influenced by the Greta Effect.

No Birthday Cake

Thunberg made the trip to Davos just two weeks after her seventeenth birthday. Her birthday is January 3, and in 2020 that fell on a Friday. It meant that Thunberg skipped school that day and, as she had done for most Fridays for more than a year, toted her "School Strike for the Climate" sign to the Parliament House in Stockholm. It was, in fact, the seventy-second consecutive Friday that either Thunberg or other climate activists had protested in front of Parliament House.

Climate Activism and the VSCO Girls

Anybody who has scanned through the social media posts of climate activists has undoubtedly come across photos of so-called VSCO girls participating in the protests. (VSCO refers to a photo editing application that is pronounced "visco.") VSCO girls are often dressed in trendy clothes—many appear as though they are on their way to the beach—and they always appear to be having a good time. But VSCO girls are very serious when it comes to the climate crisis. For years, teenage girls have found that their demands are often ignored by those in power. Many teenage girls, among them the VSCO girls, feel emboldened by Greta Thunberg and believe now that they, too, can make a difference.

Says journalist Kate Aronoff, "It's not as if all VSCO girls are sleeper climate champions. But as climate organizing has come to involve more and more people, it's sucking the trends of the day up with it, as those trends in turn reflect the concerns and anxieties of the generation from which they've sprouted." Abby Leedy, the eighteen-year-old co-coordinator of Sunrise Movement, a Philadelphia-based environmental group, says she has also noticed that teenage girls are very involved in the climate movement. She says, "It feels less like a matter of changing their minds about the correct course of action and more a matter of presenting people an opportunity to get involved. I'm just very excited to see more unorganized high schoolers getting involved, especially VSCO girls and other people we don't necessarily think of as being organizers."

Kate Arnoff, "Why VSCO Girls Are Going on Strike for the Climate," The Intercept, September 20, 2019. https://theintercept.com.

When reporters asked Thunberg how she planned to celebrate her birthday, the teen activist said she had no plans at all. "I'm not the kind of person who celebrates birthdays," Thunberg said. "I stand here striking from 8 a.m. until 3 p.m. as usual. Then I'll go home. I won't have a birthday cake but we'll have a dinner."[62]

Thunberg was also asked by the reporters to reflect on the past two years—how she had grown from a solitary climate activist to an international celebrity. Thunberg agreed that the past two years had been hectic. When she commenced her activism in 2018, she had no idea the School Strike for the Climate and the Fridays for Future campaigns would grow into international events. Nor did she expect millions of other young people would take up the cause, with many planning and orchestrating their own events. What had become clear to her, however, is that it will not be easy to get countries, businesses, and individuals to change policies and practices. But now, Thunberg added, she is more determined than ever to fight for the future of the earth. And, she told the reporters, she intends to devote the rest of her life to the cause.

Source Notes

Introduction: Greta Thunberg: *Time*'s Person of the Year

1. Edward Felsenthal, "The Choice," *Time*, December 23–December 30, 2019, p. 48.
2. Quoted in Charlotte Alter, Susan Haynes, and Justin Worland, "The Conscience," *Time*, December 23–December 30, 2019, p. 50.
3. Elizabeth Weise, "'How Dare You?' Read Greta Thunberg's Emotional Climate Change Speech to UN and World Leaders," *USA Today*, September 23, 2018. www.usatoday.com.
4. Quoted in Kerry Flynn, "*Time* Person of the Year: Climate Crisis Activist Greta Thunberg," CNN, December 11, 2019. www.cnn.com.

Chapter One: The Climate Crisis Comes to Stockholm

5. Quoted in Amelia Tait, "Greta Thunberg: How One Teenager Became the Voice of the Planet," *Wired*, June 6, 2019. www.wired.co.uk.
6. Quoted in Michael Part, *The Greta Thunberg Story: Being Different Is a Superpower*. Beverly Hills, CA: Sole Books, 2019, p. 17.
7. Quoted in Alter, Haynes, and Worland, "The Conscience," p. 58.
8. Quoted in Alter, Haynes, and Worland, "The Conscience," p. 58.
9. Quoted in Andrew C. Revkin, "Special Report: Endless Summer—Living with the Greenhouse Effect," *Discover*, June 23, 2008. www.discovermagazine.com.

10. Quoted in Ian Sample, "The Father of Climate Change," *The Guardian*, June 30, 2005. www.theguardian.com.

11. Swedish Meteorological and Hydrological Institute, "Heatwave in May 2018: 'It was Unusually Warm; Exceptional, Even,'" July 17, 2018. www.smhi.se.

12. Quoted in Part, *The Greta Thunberg Story*, pp. 57–58.

Chapter Two: School Strike for the Climate

13. Quoted in Part, *The Greta Thunberg Story*, p. 73.

14. Quoted in Tait, "Greta Thunberg.

15. Quoted in Tait, "Greta Thunberg."

16. Quoted in Milan Schreuer, Elian Peltier, and Christopher F. Schuetze, "Teenagers Emerge as a Force in Climate Protests Across Europe," *New York Times*, January 31, 2019. www.nytimes.com.

17. Quoted in Schreuer, Peltier, and Schuetze, "Teenagers Emerge as a Force in Climate Protests Across Europe."

18. Greta Thunberg, *No One Is Too Small to Make a Difference*. New York: Penguin, 2019, pp. 5–6.

19. Quoted in John Sutter and Lawrence Davidson, "Teen Tells Climate Negotiators They Aren't Mature Enough," CNN, December 17, 2018. www.cnn.com.

20. Quoted in Sutter and Davidson, "Teen Tells Climate Negotiators They Aren't Mature Enough."

21. Quoted in James Workman, "'Our House Is on Fire,' 16-Year-Old Greta Thunberg Wants Action," World Economic Forum, January 25, 2019. www.weforum.org.

22. Quoted in Sarah Kaplan, "How a 7th-Grader's Strike Against Climate Change Exploded into a Movement," *Washington Post*, February 16, 2019. www.washingtonpost.com.

23. Quoted in Eleanor Goldberg Fox, "A 10-Year-Old Climate Activist with Asperger's Inspired by Greta Thunberg 'Radicalized' His Own Mom," MSN, September 25, 2019. www.msn.com.

24. Quoted in Harmeet Kaur, "She's 12 and She's Trying to Save the World by Skipping School," CNN, March 15, 2019. www.cnn.com.

25. Quoted in Rachel Becker, "Students 'Strike for Climate' Across the United States," The Verge, March 15, 2019. www.theverge.com.

26. Quoted in Grace McGettigan, "No Toilet, No Shower and Sea Sickness: Greta Thunberg Sets Sail for New York," *Image*, August 14, 2019. www.image.ie.

27. Quoted in Tara Law, "Climate Activist Greta Thunberg, 16, Arrives in New York After Sailing Across the Atlantic," *Time*, August 28, 2019. https://time.com.

28. Quoted in Anne Barnard and James Barron, "Climate Strike N.Y.C.: Young Crowds Demand Action, Welcome Greta Thunberg," *New York Times*, September 20, 2019. www.nytimes.com.

29. National Public Radio, "Transcript: Greta Thunberg's Speech at the UN Climate Action Summit," September 23, 2019. www.npr.org.

Chapter Three: Standing Up to the Climate Change Deniers

30. James Inhofe, "Science of Climate Change," *Congressional Record*, July 28, 2003. www.govinfo.gov.

31. Quoted in Samantha Grasso, "*Fox & Friends* Is Terrified of Greta Thunberg," September 23, 2019. https://splinternews.com.

32. Quoted in Grasso, "*Fox & Friends Is Terrified of Greta Thunberg*."

33. Quoted in Justin Baragona and Maxwell Tani, "Fox News Guest Calls Greta Thunberg 'Mentally Ill Swedish Child' as Right Wing Unleashes on Climate Activist," *Daily Beast*, September 24, 2019. www.thedailybeast.com.

34. Quoted in Allyson Chiu, "A Fox News Guest Called Greta Thunberg 'Mentally Ill.' The Network Apologized for the 'Disgraceful' Comment," *Washington Post*, September 24, 2019. www.washingtonpost.com.

35. Quoted in Jenna Amatulli, "Laura Ingraham Compared Teen-age Activist Greta Thunberg to '*Children of the Corn*,'" *Huffpost*, September 24, 2019. www.huffpost.com.

36. Quoted in Nicholas Wu, "Laura Ingraham Compares Greta Thunberg, Climate Activists to '*Children of the Corn*.'" *USA Today*, September 24, 2019. www.usatoday.com.

37. Bill Wirtz, "By All Means, Let's Criticize Greta Thunberg," *American Conservative*, September 25, 2019. www.theamericanconservative.com.

38. Quoted in Part, *The Greta Thunberg Story*, p. 102.

39. Quoted in Robert Williams, "French Billionaire Arnault Calls Greta Thunberg 'Demoralizing,'" September 25, 2019. www.bloomberg.com.

40. Quoted in Hiroko Tabuchi, "'Worse than Anyone Expected': Air Travel Emissions Vastly Outpace Predictions," *New York Times*, September 19, 2019. www.nytimes.com.

41. Quoted in Adam Vaughan, "Aviation Chief Criticizes Greta Thunberg and 'Flight-Shaming' Movement," *New Scientist*, December 31, 2019. www.newscientist.com.

42. Quoted in Vaughan, "Aviation Chief."

43. Quoted in Tom Phillips, "Greta Thunberg Labeled a 'Brat' by Brazil's Far-Right Leader Jair Bolsonaro," *The Guardian*, December 10, 2019. www.theguardian.com.

44. Quoted in Deutsche Welle, "Australia Fires: Prime Minister Defends Climate Policy After Greta Thunberg Criticism," December 23, 2019. www.dw.com.

45. Quoted in James Walker, "Australian Prime Minister Responds to Greta Thunberg's Bushfires Tweet: 'I'm Not Here to Try and Impress People Overseas,'" *Newsweek*, December 23, 2019. www.newsweek.com.

46. Quoted in Chris Cillizza, "We Should All Be Appalled by Donald Trump's Tweet About Greta Thunberg," CNN, December 13, 2019. www.cnn.com.

47. Quoted in Catherine Thorbecke, "Greta Thunberg 'Wouldn't Have Wasted My Time' Talking to President Trump About Climate Change," ABC News, December 30, 2019. https://abcnews.go.com.

48. Quoted in Thorbecke, "Greta Thunberg 'Wouldn't Have Wasted My Time' Talking to President Trump About Climate Change."

Chapter Four: The Greta Effect

49. Quoted in Christopher Reynolds, "Canadian Airlines Feel the Pressure of Flight Shaming and the 'Greta Effect,'" Global News, January 19, 2020. https://globalnews.ca.

50. Quoted in Hanna Hoikkala and Niklas Magnusson, "As 'Flying Shame' Grips Sweden, SAS Ups Stakes in Climate Battle," Bloomberg, April 14, 2019. www.bloomberg.com.

51. Quoted in Katherine Dunn, "Flight Shame Is 'Our Biggest Challenge,' Air France CEO Says," *Fortune*, November 18, 2019. https://fortune.com.

52. Quoted in Sandra Laville, "'Greta Thunberg Effect' Driving Growth in Carbon Dioxide Offsetting," *The Guardian*, November 8, 2019. www.theguardian.com.

53. Sally Ho, "Major Increase in Carbon Dioxide Offsetting Thanks to 'Greta Thunberg Effect,'" Green Queen, November 12, 2019. www.greenqueen.com.

54. Quoted in Will Bunch, "These Pesky Teenagers Have a Scheme for Saving Planet Earth. It Drops in September," *Philadelphia Inquirer*, August 8, 2019. www.inquirer.com.

55. Quoted in Andrea Germanos, "'We Are Unstoppable, Another World Is Possible!' Young Climate Activists Storm COP 25 Stage," December 11, 2019. www.commondreams.org.

56. Quoted in Anna Schori, "When Alexandria Ocasio-Cortez Met Greta Thunberg: 'Hope Is Contagious,'" *The Guardian*, June 29, 2019. www.theguardian.com.

57. Quoted in Schori, "When Alexandria Ocasio-Cortez Met Greta Thunberg."

58. Quoted in James Keaten, "Davos Chief Welcomes Both Trump, Thunberg," *Philadelphia Inquirer*, January 20, 2020. www.inquirer.com.

59. Quoted in Rick Noack, "Thunberg: 'Our House Is Still on Fire,'" *Philadelphia Inquirer*, January 22, 2020. www.inquirer.com.

60. Quoted in Alexandra Alper and Luke Baker, "Trump Laments Missing Davos Star Greta's Speech," Reuters, January 22, 2020. www.reuters.com.
61. Quoted in John Bowden, "Ivanka Trump Refuses to Criticize Greta Thunberg: 'She's Elevated Awareness,'" *The Hill*, January 22, 2020. https://thehill.com.
62. Quoted in Colm Fulton, "Climate Strike but No Cake for Greta Thunberg as She Turns 17," Reuters, January 3, 2020. www.reuters.com.

Important Events in the Life of Greta Thunberg

2003
January 3: Greta Thunberg is born in Stockholm, Sweden.

2015
May 21: Thunberg's mother, opera star Malena Ernman, discloses in a newspaper interview that her daughter has been diagnosed with Asperger's syndrome.

2018
May: Thunberg wins an essay contest sponsored by a Stockholm newspaper that invited students to write about the dangers of climate change.

August 20: Thunberg skips school to begin her School Strike for the Climate protest in front of Parliament House in Stockholm.

September 9: Thunberg begins the Fridays for Future protest, skipping school each Friday to campaign against climate change.

October 31: Thunberg addresses the Extinction Rebellion protest in London, England.

December 3: Thunberg addresses the UN Climate Change Conference in Katowice, Poland.

2019
January 24: Thunberg addresses the World Economic Forum in Davos, Switzerland.

March 14: Three members of the Norwegian parliament nominate Thunberg for the Nobel Peace Prize.

March 15: An estimated 1.6 million students worldwide skip school to take part in a climate strike.

August 14: Thunberg boards the sailing ship *Malizia II* for a fifteen-day voyage to New York City to give a speech before the United Nations.

September 23: Thunberg speaks before the UN Climate Action Summit.

December 11: *Time* magazine selects Thunberg as its Person of the Year.

December 12: US President Donald Trump mocks Thunberg in a Twitter post.

2020

January 3: Thunberg celebrates her seventeenth birthday by participating in a Fridays for Future protest in front of Sweden's Parliament House.

For Further Research

Books

Valentina Camerini, *Greta's Story: The Schoolgirl Who Went on Strike to Save the Planet.* London: Simon & Schuster UK, 2019.

Al Gore, *An Inconvenient Sequel: Truth to Power, Your Action Handbook to Learn the Science, Find Your Voice, and Help Solve the Climate Crisis*. New York: Rodale Books, 2017.

Don Nardo, *Planet Under Siege: Climate Change*. San Diego, CA: ReferencePoint, 2020.

Michael Part, *The Greta Thunberg Story: Being Different Is a Superpower*. Beverly Hills, CA: Sole Books, 2019.

Greta Thunberg, *No One Is Too Small to Make a Difference*. New York: Penguin Books, 2019.

Greta Thunberg, Svante Thunberg, Malena Ernman, and Beata Ernman, *Our House Is on Fire: Scenes of a Family and a Planet in Crisis*. New York: Penguin Books, 2020.

Internet Sources

Sarah Kaplan, "How a 7th-Grader's Strike Against Climate Change Exploded into a Movement," *Washington Post*, February 16, 2019. www.washingtonpost.com.

National Public Radio, "Transcript: Greta Thunberg's Speech at the UN Climate Action Summit," September 23, 2019. www.npr.org.

Anna Schori, "When Alexandria Ocasio-Cortez Met Greta Thunberg: 'Hope Is Contagious,'" *The Guardian*, June 29, 2019. www.theguardian.com.

Milan Schreuer, Elian Peltier, and Christopher F. Schuetze, "Teenagers Emerge as a Force in Climate Protests Across Europe," *New York Times*, January 31, 2019. www.nytimes.com.

Amelia Tait, "Greta Thunberg: How One Teenager Became the Voice of the Planet," *Wired*, June 6, 2019. www.wired.co.uk.

Websites

Committee for a Constructive Tomorrow (CFACT)
www.cfact.org

CFACT's mission is to question the science that has reported the earth's warming climate. The group's cfact.org website includes a number of news reports questioning the authenticity of climate science. By accessing the "Collegians" link on the website, visitors can read about efforts by college students to oppose climate activists on their campuses.

Extinction Rebellion—https://rebellion.earth

The British group, which hosted a speech by Greta Thunberg in 2018, has often resorted to civil disobedience to protest against climate change. Visitors to the group's website can find videos of the group's protests, news accounts of speeches delivered by activists, including Thunberg, and read statements by Extinction Rebellion officials commenting on the issue of climate change.

Fridays for Future—www.fridaysforfuture.org

The website reports on Fridays for Future protests throughout the world. Visitors to the website can find statistics on the number of activists who have participated in the protests, a world map displaying cities where the protests have been held, and instructions for activists on how to stage Fridays for Future protests.

Greta Thunberg: Climate Activist
www.ted.com/speakers/greta_thunberg

The website is sponsored by TED Conferences, a media outlet that makes speeches by newsmakers available to the public. The site includes a video of Greta Thunberg's "TED Talk" on climate activism, which she delivered in January 2019.

Time Person of the Year: Greta Thunberg

https://time.com/person-of-the-year-2019-greta-thunberg

Time's website explains why the magazine selected Greta Thunberg as its Person of the Year in 2019. The website includes the stories about Thunberg published in the print version of the magazine as well as numerous photos of Thunberg and other young people attending climate rallies.

UN Framework Convention on Climate Change

https://unfccc.int/cop25

The UN organization that invited Greta Thunberg to address its delegates focuses on reducing greenhouse gas emissions. By accessing the "Topics" tab on the organization's website, students can find reports on how new technology can reduce the use of fossil fuels as well as how schools can teach young people how they can reduce their carbon impact.

US Environmental Protection Agency—www.epa.gov

The US government's chief environmental watchdog agency provides many resources on its website explaining climate change. By entering "climate change" into the website's search engine, students can find reports on how climate change is measured, the effects of climate change on wildlife, and other impacts of climate change on life on earth.

US Representative Alexandria Ocasio-Cortez

https://ocasio-cortez.house.gov

The congresswoman from New York City is the author of the Green New Deal, legislation that would require dramatic cuts in greenhouse gas emissions in the United States. By accessing the link to "Issues" on the congresswoman's website, students can download copies of the US House bill Ocasio-Cortez has written to address climate change.

Wildfires in Australia

https://earthobservatory.nasa.gov/images
/event/145600/wildfires-in-australia

Maintained by the National Aeronautics and Space Administration (NASA), the website includes images made by American satellites of the wildfires that swept through Australia in late 2019 and early 2020. Students can access numerous images, each of which are provided with explanations of the climate conditions that led to the fires.

World Economic Forum USA—www.weforum.org

The website for the American headquarters of the Swiss-based organization of world business leaders provides many resources on how the group is addressing climate change. By accessing the "Themes" link on the website, students can review numerous essays by WEF officials on reversing the effects of climate change.

Index

Picture Credits

About the Author

Hal Marcovitz is a former newspaper reporter and columnist who has written more than two hundred books for young readers. He makes his home in Chalfont, Pennsylvania.